The Ultim

Team Building

Quickly Increase Team Building And Project Management Skills For Better Employee Engagement, Motivation, Production, And Workplace Morale!

Ryan Cooper

STOP!!! Before you read any further....Would you like to know the Secrets of Transforming your life, overcome insecurities, develop leadership skills, and undeniable confidence in your personal, professional, and relationship life?

If your answer is yes, then you are not alone. Thousands of people are looking for the secret to have unstoppable confidence and self-driven power in all areas of their lives.

If you have been searching for these answers without much luck, you're in the right place!

Not only will you gain incredible insight in this book, but because I want to make sure to give you as much value as possible, right now for a limited time you can get full **100% FREE access to a VIP bonus EBook** entitled **LIMITLESS ENERGY!**

Just Go Here For Free Instant Access:

www.PotentialRise.com

Legal Notice

Disclaimer Notice

conditions change, the author and publisher reserve the right to alter and update the information contained herein on the new conditions whenever they see applicable.

Table Of Contents

Introduction

I want to thank you and congratulate you for purchasing the book, *"Team Building: The Ultimate Team Building Guide! - Quickly Increase Team Building And Project Management Skills For Better Employee Engagement, Motivation, Production, And Workplace Morale!"*

This "Team Building" book contains proven steps and strategies on how to quickly win over the confidence of your current team and gain the respect of new members. You will learn the basics of proper team structures and all the details of how to properly motivate for the best output of the team and each individual!

You will also learn many other skills that will help you in your abilities to lead and manage this team, such as but not limited to the following:

- How to make team building sessions work for you;

- Eliminating the road blocks that can delay the progression of your team and accomplishment of its goals;

- How to build and use power rapport skills to gain confidence and respect;

- Identifying the core elements in forming the right team building structure;

- The best steps to assign leadership and management roles within your team;

- How to develop and use your leadership charisma to build the motivation of your team and to direct team members towards the accomplishment of goals;

- How to deal with difficult or mean team members, instill discipline, improve their attitude so they become productive members like the rest;

- Proven ways on how to boost team productivity and morale;

- How to develop a culture of excellence and collaboration through enhanced leadership skills;

- You will also find creative tips to increase engagement as well as boost and sustain motivation of your team members.

All these and more await you with the purchase of this book and reading its content.

Thanks again for purchasing this book, I hope you enjoy it!

Chapter 1: Understanding The Complications Of Team Building

Understand that team building is not an overnight process. You cannot just hold a team building session for you and your staff and expect it to be an instant solution for all members to work well together. It is, however, a powerful solution and a continuing process when applied correctly.

Making the Team Building Session Work for You

In this chapter, let us unlock the difficulties of team building in order for you to do it the right way and benefit the most from its power. It is also important to realize the fact no two companies or organizations have exactly the same needs. As such, your team building session and exercises should match your organization's unique situation.

Relative to the foregoing, to make team building sessions and exercises work for your organization, they should be able to address the root of why the members are not behaving and working as one team. The team building itself should be able to strengthen the "sense of team" in each of the employees of your organization, and this is a continuing process, not just a one-time event.

Four Team Building Difficulties to Unlock

Having said that, here are five team-building difficulties to unlock:

1. Lack of Awareness and Understanding – often, the source of conflict among members is they do not understand clearly their roles, the goals of the team, as well as the code of conduct and cooperation.

    As a result, team members usually resort to finger pointing, blaming one another, using scapegoats, and being hypercritical of one another's actions and ways.

Increasing their level of awareness and understanding of their roles, goals, and implementing a code of conduct and cooperation will enable team members to de-focus on others and focus on themselves.

2. Lack of Conversational Capacity – Team issues usually escalate during critical times or when under pressure. The major cause is the lack of conversational capacity. The Weber Consulting defines this as the team's ability to engage in an open discussion without prejudices or biases.

   Teams with high conversational capacity may still disagree but their disagreements are part of resolving the issue. Teams with low conversational capacity are more likely to disagree often and over trivial matters that affect productivity and performance.

3. Misplaced Goals – while the spirit of competition may spark or stimulate enthusiasm among your employees, your team building goals should refrain from centering on competition. Instead of competition, encourage and inspire your employees to cooperate.

   While it is important to improve individual competencies, the team members should not attempt to outshine one another. They should be able to respect the identity of their team, and pull each other up to meet team goals. The interests of the team should be more valuable than self-interests.

4. Management Attitude – admit it or not, but most times, the management look at team building as the process to enable staff to change, improve, and work with one another cohesively. Management rarely, if they do, include themselves in the picture.

   The thing is that the participation of the manager or the leader is the most critical. Any organization cannot build a solid team unless the management is willing to look into its own contributions and improve as necessary.

Chapter 2: How To Use Power Rapport Building Skills To Gain Confidence In Your Current Team And Gain The Respect Of New Team Members

In the previous chapter, we have unlocked the difficulties that make team building a rather complicated process. In this chapter, we will look into the relevance of building rapport and the ways you can use it to increase your confidence in your present team and gain the respect of new team.

Why Building Rapport Is Important

If you wish to build your team, build rapport first. Rapport building is crucial primarily for two major things: (1) trust and (2) influence. Without rapport, it will be extremely difficult for team members to trust one another, and for the management to influence their staff. Without rapport, the members will remain disconnected.

Here are the top reasons why you need to develop your power rapport building skills:

- It will be easier for you to engage your team members to work cooperatively and enhance their competencies to achieve team goals.

- You will connect more easily and quickly to enjoy a solid relationship with the members of your present team and new team. With a solid relationship, you will be able to get your team members to respond to your calls to action effortlessly.

- Studies show that employees who enjoy a solid and comfortable relationship with one another and with the management are happier, and this translates to increase in productivity.

Using Power Rapport Building Skills for Confidence

Here are powerful ways you use your rapport building skills to gain confidence:

- Use it to calm the tension that may exist in your present team or when meeting members of a new team. Your rapport building skills come in handy when you need to break the ice.

- Using your skills, match how the members communicate both verbally and non-verbally. It is critical that you use the appropriate non-verbal signals, as more often than not, these signals have more persuasive and convincing powers than verbal communication has.

- Engage in active listening. You can acquire and hone this skill through practice. It also involves combing other rapport skills such as verbal and non-verbal signals to show the speaker or the member you are communicating with that you are actively listening to what he or she has to say. Examples are the following: maintaining eye contact and nodding your head (non-verbal) or saying "yes" or "uh huh" or "hmm" (verbal).

- Develop and maintain the right attitude such as the following:

  - Respecting your team members
  - Recognizing and responding to what your team members have to say whether they express it verbally or non-verbally
  - Reassuring the members that they can trust you and that they can feel comfortable with you
  - Fulfilling your responsibility as member of the team

Chapter 3: Key Elements In Forming The Proper Team Building Structure For Your Organization, And Why It Is Important To Have Structure

For any team to work best, it has to be orderly. To put order into your team, it has to have a structure. In this chapter, you will learn about the importance of structure in team building and the core elements in forming the proper team building structure.

What is Structure in Team Building

In teambuilding, you define structure as the inner order that will make the process of team building enjoyable and fun without playing games. You cannot do things just for creating structure and expect them to work. In order to benefit, you need to put together the right elements and see to it that the structure:

- Fits the objectives of the team best
- Is coherent, clear, and reasonable for the team members
- Does not confuse the members believing that efforts and results are identical

In general, you will find three kinds of team structure, all of which will produce results if you choose the best fit and you use it correctly. These are the following:

1. Tactical or Strategic Team Structure – is best for clarity. There is a clear definition of roles and norms in achieving the strategic goals of the team.

2. Problem Solving Team Structure – develops and nurtures trust among team members. Together, team members focus on finding the best resolution where the team values the contributions of each member.

3. Creative Team Structure – focuses on independence where team members can engage in casual communication in arriving at the results.

Why Is It Important to Have a Team Building Structure

Structure is important in team building primarily because:

- It allows the team members to understand their roles and accountabilities clearly.
- You will be able to improve the communication process and flow in the presence of a structure.
- You can have the framework for establishing metrics that will help you in measuring and monitoring individual and group performance of your team.
- It enables you to decide based on facts.

Core Elements in Forming the Proper Team Building Structure

To form the proper team building structure, you must see to it that it consists of the following core elements:

- Mission Statement– this element describes the purpose of the team as aligned to the overall mission statement of the company

- Goals, Objectives, and Targets – will make the team building process measurable ad quantifiable. They have to be S.M.A.R.T.E.R (specific, measurable, achievable, realistic, time-bounded, evaluable, and re-doable)

- Rules and Procedures – that will enable team members to avoid unnecessary conflicts and frustrations.

- Process Flow- determines roles and responsibilities as well as accountabilities of each member of the team.

- Skills and Competencies – each team member must be equipped with the right skills and competencies to perform their roles and responsibilities.

The structure has to be result-oriented whether in performing team and individual tasks (to do the things they need to do) or in maintaining the solid connection of the team (making sure that they contribute to the cohesiveness of the team).

Chapter 4: Guidelines For Assigning Different Leadership And Management Roles Within Your Team's Structure

You have learned earlier that structure in building a team is important for the members to become aware of, recognize, and understand their respective roles. There are various roles within your team and these include leadership and management.

This chapter will provide you the guidelines on how to assign different leadership and management roles within your team's structure.

Understanding the Difference between Leadership and Management

First, you need to understand that leadership and management, while they co-exist and in many ways similar to each other, are two different concepts. Here are a few of the remarkable differences between the two:

- Leadership inspires the team to work together as one in achieving goals. Management, on the other hand, oversees and directs the implementation of the strategy to achieve team goals. Perhaps this difference is the basis for the adage that "all leaders are also managers, but not all managers are leaders".

- In achieving team goals or getting to the destination, leaders focus on opportunities and potentials for growth and development while managers focus on the bottom lines. Hence, managers will seldom challenge the status quo unlike leaders.

- Leaders normally tap the potentials of all team members with the goal of bringing out the best in each. Managers, meanwhile, limit the involvement of the members to only those who are concerned or to those with "the need to know".

Identifying What the Team Needs to Accomplish

Team goals will also serve as basis for assigning leadership and manager roles within the structure of your team. For instance, management is often associated with businesses and corporations since the goals are usually increasing the bottom lines or earning high returns on investment. Leadership meanwhile is closely associated with governments since the goals involve inspiring the constituents and encouraging their participation.

Determining the Skills Required

Once you have identified the goals and tasks, the next thing to do is to identify the skills necessary for the accomplishment of these goals/tasks. You also have to familiarize yourself with the skills of your team members, as well as their attitude, to determine what leadership and management roles fit members best.

Assigning Roles Accordingly

Match the skills needed for the accomplishment of the tasks or goals and the skills of your members. Assign roles accordingly, but make sure that:

- The assignment of roles meets the approval of your team.
- Each of your team members are satisfied with the roles assigned to them.

Assigning leadership and management roles is something that you do very carefully since it can considerably affect team performance. If you are able to find the right match, you can expect your team to perform higher than the standards. Aim for a combination of leader-manager roles.

Chapter 5: Understanding The Role That Charisma Can Play In Your Ability To Motivate And Direct Your Employees

There is no doubt that charisma is one effective way to motivate and direct your employees to perform their roles and functions and work together as a team. However, you must know how to use your charisma. To do this, it is crucial that you understand the role it plays in your ability to lead your team. Let us find out in this chapter.

What It Is

In the context of team building and leadership, charisma is your influence as a leader that inspires team members to work together to reach team goals. Being a charismatic leader is important since he or she inspires the team to work enthusiastically and deliver consistent performance all the way to its destination of success.

Charisma is like a magnet. When you have it as a leader, your belief, e.g. work ethics, easily resonate with your employees. Under a charismatic leadership, there is higher employee engagement that results with greater productivity for the team and the company or organization in general.

Do You Need It?

You need charisma to attract people, build rapport, and nurture a mutually beneficial relationship with them. If you have it, it is easy for your employees to have faith in your leadership that you can bring out the best in your people.

The Role of Charisma

Charisma plays a decisive role in your ability to motivate, inspire, guide, and direct your people towards achieving team goals by giving their best. Your employees look up to you for inspiration and motivation that they develop and maintain the right attitude and mindset towards their work, functions, and own roles in the team.

Contrary to common belief, you can always develop charisma and present your employees your charismatic message. Here's how.

- Know the characteristics necessary for charismatic leadership, and develop or enhance it. The Harvard Business Review categorizes these into the following: (a) confidence, (b) personality, and (c) style.

  Specific characteristics common to charismatic leaders are the following: (a) maturity through experience that charismatic leaders can easily survive business challenges such as financial downturns; (b) exceptional verbal and non-verbal communication skills; (c) they listen to their people with empathy and they exercise humility; (d) a charismatic leader is a person of substance that words and actions match.

- Explaining to your employees clearly what actions you expect from each of them and how important these actions are in accomplishing team goals. You can only expect them to deliver their best if your employees know and understand clear the actions they need to take.

- Recognize the power of emotions, use it to bring out the best in your people, but be careful not to play with their emotions. Be careful with what you say and how you say it, as people will remember it best with how you made them feel. Use positive words to evoke positive emotions in your employees. Genuine praise as necessary is one good example.

Use charisma to inspire your employees. It should be able to motivate them and support your beliefs and principles, but not to the point of hero-worshiping you. The goal is to provide inspiration for team members and sustain their motivation in delivering their best performance both as individuals and as team members.

Chapter 6 Tips For Dealing With Difficult People/Mean People In The Workplace And How To Discipline Them Properly

Conflicts and disagreements are normal occurrences in any organizations or companies. It becomes too much to handle with the presence of difficult people or mean people in the workplace. They have a way of making things worse, but it does not mean you will just let them do their thing especially since it can affect team performance.

In this chapter, you will learn how to deal with this kind of people and how to discipline them properly.

Dealing with Mean Employees

The first thing you need to do is to understand why you should take the necessary actions to deal with mean employees, especially when they are part of your team. The top reasons are:

- These people can hinder the growth and productivity of the team
- They become your excess baggage that can weigh your team down
- Difficult people tend to drain the energy of other members and influence them negatively

Next is to find out what is the root of their meanness. There is always wisdom to the saying that the best resolution is one that addresses the root of the problem. This could be any of the following:

- Stress and anxiety whether from pressures at work or at home
- Negative experience in the past
- Lack of motivation or de-motivation

- Differences in personality and work ethics
- Undefined or unclear roles that make these people feel threatened or see other members as threat

Consider these steps in handling difficult/mean people in your team:

1. Accept that conflict exists and that there is a problem within your team that needs the best resolution. Do not delay efforts in finding the root of the problem as it will lead you to the right solution.

2. Focus on the misconduct or negative behavior. Never attack the character of the person, as it will only aggravate the situation and may drive the person to display his or her worst behavior. By focusing on the misconduct, you will also be able to look at the problem with objectivity and avoid your biases and prejudice.

3. Once you are able to determine the root, find what your options are in resolving the problem, and choose what is best for the team. Implement the solution accordingly.

Disciplining Them Properly

The premise for discipline is that the actions are meant to correct the misconduct or misbehavior and not to punish the person. It is also assumed that at the onset, the team is aware that there exists a code of conduct and ethical behavior that they need to follow and observe. With these, here is how to discipline difficult/mean people in your team:

- Remind the person of the code of conduct and any other specific rules and regulations that the entire team has agreed to follow.

- Help the person realize how the misconduct on his/her part is negatively affecting (a) his/her career; and (b) the team where he/she belongs.

- Respect the person's feelings and dignity. Be careful not to abuse your authority when instilling discipline, and never act and decide on the basis of your biases and prejudices.

- Gather all information that you can use to come up with an objective decision. Make sure that you have factual information and not based on hearsays. It is also best to document the information you have gathered.

- Be sure to follow protocol and due process. The person has to know that his or her behavior is hurting not only his or her performance of his or her duties and responsibilities, but also that of the other team members'. Guide the person to correct his or her misdemeanor and monitor the progress.

- Provide the person with all the opportunities to improve his or her conduct, and guide the person through it. If the person shows no improvement despite all efforts, or if you have exhausted all options in disciplining the person to no avail, then it's time to let go and apply the necessary action which may include termination of his or her employment.

Chapter 7: How To Increase Production From Your Employees While Also Increasing Overall Workplace Morale

Productivity and morale are crucial factors in ensuring team growth and development. When morale is high, team members tend to deliver their best performance that also results in an increase in productivity. Similarly, when a team is productive, it radiates positive energy that boosts the overall morale in the workplace.

In this chapter, you will discover how to increase the productivity of your team members that will also increase the overall workplace morale.

Increasing Productivity of the Team

Studies show that among the factors that impacts on team productivity, the most crucial is communication. Effective communication results in increase in productivity, while the lack of communication or miscommunication either stalls or lowers productivity.

This is because more often than not, conflict among team members arises when:

- Team members are not aware of or they do not clearly understand what is expected of them;

- They find it difficult to verbalize what their needs are;

- They can hardly connect their individual needs to the needs of their team to the needs of the entire organization;

- The members only focus on their own interests instead of upholding the interests of the team.

The solution is to ensure that you have an effective and efficient communication in place that will:

- Develop and maintain trust and respect among the team members;
- Enable your members to realize the value of upholding the team's interests over individual interests;
- Empower your team members to perform their roles with much confidence;
- Help the team to avoid confusion and unnecessary conflicts that hinder productivity;
- Provide clear directions and remove roadblocks in achieving your targets.

Increasing Overall Workplace Morale

Effective communication does not only make team members more productive, but it can also boost their morale and increase the overall morale of the company. Therefore, leaders and managers have the responsibility to boost the morale of their staff or team members. Here are some proven ways that will result in increases in morale and productivity:

- Be sure that you communicate clear instructions, directives, procedures, or rules, for the tasks that team members have to do or accomplish.

- See to it that team members maintain an open line of communication that puts high premium on trust and respect.

- Increase the involvement and engagement of your team members and make them an integral component of the decision making process. You have to set the boundaries though and communicate the same clearly to your people.

Further, be sure that you distribute the tasks equally among the team members and consider their skills in assigning them their tasks or workload. Encourage a culture of excellence, and at the same time find ways to ensure that your team members enjoy the benefits of good work-life balance.

Chapter 8: How To Enhance Your Leadership Skills For Exceptional Team Building And Project Management

If you see the merit of building your team, it is worth to build it well. To do this, you need to put your leadership skills at work. In this chapter, you will learn how to enhance your leadership skills to come up with outstanding team building and project management.

Core Skills You Need as a Leader

Here are the essential leadership skills that you need for exceptional team building and project management:

- Communication skills – this top the list of the core skills necessary to become the best team builder and project manager. You must have the ability to communicate clearly the vision, mission, goals, objective, and targets to your members.

- Strategic and Critical Thinking skills – the best leader and manager has the ability to think critically and strategically to direct the team to the right path towards reaching the destination of success. The leader-manager is responsible for conceptualizing strategies and techniques to reach goals while using resources effectively, efficiently, and prudently.

- Problem Solving skills – as a leader-manager, you have to be able to not only recognize problems as they arise, but also to anticipate, predict, or foresee potential problems that may occur in the future. Along with this, you should be able to find the best solutions that will address the root of the problem, and plan your contingencies as well as to minimize or eliminate risks.

How to Enhance Your Skills

Here are proven ways to enhance your core skills as a leader-manager:

Communication Skills

- Use appropriate verbal and non-verbal signals in communicating. Keep your words positive even when you have to discipline mean people in your team. Praise in public and reprimand in private.

- As much as possible, personalize your communication such as limiting issuance of memorandum, but instead engaging your team members to participate in focus group discussions and conversations. You also have to encourage your team to speak the raw truth and not its sanitized version.

Strategic/Critical Thinking Skills

- Practice looking at the big picture. Think long-term rather than short-term. Learn how to evaluate the implication of your decisions, and see how your decisions will impact on not just a particular situation, but also more than that.

- Develop the good habit of thinking clearly and using your good judgment. It also helps that you learn how to discern, as there are times that boundaries are not clearly set or may overlap.

Problem Solving

- Problem solving skills require an analytical mind. You have to learn how to analyze both quantitatively or qualitatively. Practice the habit of asking questions to extract necessary and relevant information.
- When a problem presents itself, always get to the root. Explore your options in solving the problem. Choose the option that will prevent the problem to resurface or recur and one that is most beneficial to the entire team.

Chapter 9: Creativity Tips To Increase Employee Engagement And Motivation

In this chapter, you will get to know and follow creativity tips meant to increase team member engagement and motivation in the workplace. Most of these tips come from team building and project management experts based from their own experiences.

Tips to Increase Employee Engagement

It pays a lot when members of your team trust your leadership and management style. To earn their trust, it is crucial that you build rapport and nurture your relationship with your team. There are many ways to build rapport and nurture employee relationship, and some of the best are also creative ways to do so. Here are examples:

- Share your success story, and then encourage your team members to write and share their own success stories. Together, conceptualize the success story of your team and then connect it with how your team can contribute to the overall success of the company.

- Engage your team members in brain storming more often. It does not have to be serious and boring. You can make it fun and interesting, but not to the point of playing and taking your responsibilities lightly.

Create a structure where you can reward best practices and excellent performances, and coach or counsel those that need improvement. In building a culture of excellence for your team, you also have to create the culture of participation, involvement, and engagement.

Here are also some expert tips to increase engagement of difficult team members:

- Identify the root of the problem and apply the best resolution as previously discussed in chapter 6.

- Use your charisma as a leader, as discussed in chapter5, to remove or lower the resistance of the difficult team member. Refrain from using negative verbal and non-verbal signals that can only increase the tendency of this member to refrain from engaging.

- Simplify the tasks of each member and make sure that each one fully understands his or her assignments, roles in the team, and significance and relevance in achieving performance targets.

- If the mean behavior stems from pressures, stresses, and inability to perform one's tasks, give the necessary tools and support to guide your member and inspire the person to contribute to the success of the team. You may also want to recommend that the person undergoes coaching and counseling as part of the solution.

- Keep an open mind and open your communication lines to encourage your team members to voice out their opinions, suggestions, and recommendations, including those things that you "need" to hear. Learn how not to take these things personally.

  Most times, employees are afraid to tell the truth for fear of losing their jobs. It is a common perception that when management hears something they do not want to hear, they get back. Therefore, people tend to sanitize what they have to say that usually results with management failing to resolve or anticipate the risks of bigger problems that can cost much for the company.

Tips to Increase Em*& ployee Motivation

Motivation is the fuel that will drive the team to perform at its peak and to sustain its performance to achieve its goals. Here are proven ways to increase team motivation:

- Make yourself readily available for your team. A good leader is the first among equals. This means that you just don't delegate tasks or order them what to do; instead you show them you are the example. What they do, you do and you are there all the time to help your team achieve its goals.

- Help your team members recognize and appreciate the value of their work and working as part of the team. If you are quick to call their attention when they commit mistakes, you must also be quick to commend them for a job well done. In other words, point out their good deeds and mistakes and the intention should always be to help them reach their full potentials as a team member.

- Make them feel their importance as team members. To quote Maya Angelou, "people will forget what you said, people will forget what you did, but people will never forget how you made them feel". There is so much wisdom to this since human beings are basically social beings that value their emotions. Pay attention to the best advertisements, they have one thing in common and that is they all appeal to the emotions of consumers.

- If you ask that your team members trust and respect you, it is both necessary and important that you trust and respect your team members first. You have to give first in order to take. These are cardinal and unwritten rules that will make anyone one of the best leaders-managers.

Increasing employee engagement and building and sustaining the motivation of the team are critical to success. You can never compromise these two critical factors without compromising the success of your company, business, or organization.

Conclusion

Thank you again for purchasing the book *"Team Building: The Ultimate Team Building Guide! - Quickly Increase Team Building And Project Management Skills For Better Employee Engagement, Motivation, Production, And Workplace Morale!"*

I am extremely excited to pass this information along to you, and I am so happy that you now have read and can hopefully implement these strategies going forward.

I hope this book was able to help you understand the dynamics of team building and how to use and implement the essential skills and strategies for team building and project management to enjoy the following results:

- Increase in team productivity
- Better engagement of team members
- Sustained motivation that will lead to team productivity
- High morale of team members

All of the above are critical factors in accomplishing team objectives and targets and in achieving smaller goals and then the ultimate goal. The things you have learned and discovered from this book will help you in creating the cultures of excellence, collaboration, and cooperation where each member of the team gives his or her best and upholds the interests of the team above his or her own.

The next step is to get started using this information and to hopefully live a happy, productive, and stress-free work-life!

Please don't be someone who just reads this information and doesn't apply it, the strategies in this book will only benefit you if you use them!

If you know of anyone else that could benefit from the information presented here please inform them of this book.

Finally, if you enjoyed this book and feel it has added value to your life in any way, please take the time to share your thoughts and post a review on Amazon. It'd be greatly appreciated!

Thank you and good luck!

Preview Of:

<u>Power Rapport Building!</u>

Advanced Power Rapport Building For Greater Influence, Romantic Intimacy, Meeting New Friends, Building Confidence, Persuasion, Networking And Career!

Introduction

I want to thank you and congratulate you for purchasing the book, *"Power Rapport Building: Advanced Power Rapport Building For Greater Influence, Romantic Intimacy, Meeting New Friends, Building Confidence, Persuasion, Networking And Career!"*.

Power Rapport Building for Transforming All Areas of Your Life!

This "Power Rapport Building" book contains proven steps and strategies on how to confidently approach and talk to anyone! Gaining the skill of building rapport will greatly enhance your ability to meet new friends, talk to or meet members of the opposite sex, increase your networking abilities for your professional life, and much more!

By using this book, you will learn basic and advanced strategies in using your charisma to start new and improve existing relationships. You can use these relationships for various life goals like improving your career, building a professional network, or finding the right person to spend the rest of your life with.

Let's start building your network today!

Thanks again for purchasing this book, I hope you enjoy it!

Chapter 1 - How Power Rapport Building Can Transform All Areas Of Your Life

Becoming socially intelligent will affect all the aspects of your life. Your career, friendly and romantic relationships, family life and your own self-image will improve after you are done with this book.

Career

The adage "It's not what you know but who you know" is applicable in almost all industries. Regardless of how good you are in your profession, if you are not skilled playing the game of office politics, you will not advance in your career.

Knowing the right people and how to get in touch with them will help you improve your chances in improving your career position. Being able to build relationships even with strangers will widen your network. The people you know may be able to help you in time of need. They may also bring you clients for your profession. For this to happen, you need to show qualities that people approve of.

Learning to build rapport will also help you when dealing with your competition. If you are competing with a colleague for example, being socially aware of the situation will prevent you from taking things personally. It will prevent you from playing dirty because you know that doing so will ultimately hurt your social image and ruin your career.

Relationships

By learning how to build rapport, you will know how to get along with people who are most important to you. You will become more sensitive with the feelings of others. You will also be able to act maturely in stressful situations.

Your partner will be one of the people who will most appreciate your social intelligence. Because you are level-headed when dealing with stressful situations, there will be fewer arguments in your relationship. If arguments do happen, you will have the presence of mind to prevent them from creating permanent damage to your relationship.

People who don't have social skills usually let their emotions run wild when in a confrontation. By learning how to build and maintain rapport, you will know how to act to prevent emotional outbursts from further ruining your relationships.

You will also be able to create connections with people in other communities that you become a member of. If you know how to build connections and its advantages, you will not shy away from social gatherings. Even if you are an introvert, you will know how to behave the right way in the presence of different types of people. In the workplace, this will encourage collaboration while in your family life; it will encourage a happy home atmosphere.

Personal Advantages

There are also a lot of personal advantages to building rapport. Shy people tend to improve their self-esteem when they begin to create relationships with new people. These small improvements become social victories that can improve their confidence.

You will also learn how to plan your social image. Having social intelligence makes you aware of your social image at all times. You always have an idea of people's impression of you. You are aware of how your actions affect your social image and you can strategize on how you can improve it to help you reach your career and personal goals.

All the other advantages mentioned above will contribute to your happiness and self-actualization. If you are in a job that requires constant interaction with people, these improvements will significantly enhance your performance.

Thanks for Previewing My Exciting Book Entitled:

"Power Rapport Building! Advanced Power Rapport Building For Greater Influence, Romantic Intimacy, Meeting New Friends, Building Confidence, Persuasion, Networking And Career!"

To purchase this book, simply go to the Amazon Kindle store and simply search:

"POWER RAPPORT BUILDING"

Then just scroll down until you see my book. You will know it is mine because you will see my name "Ryan Cooper" underneath the title.

Alternatively, you can visit my author page on Amazon to see this book and other work I have done. Thanks so much, and please don't forget your free bonuses.

DON'T LEAVE YET! - CHECK OUT YOUR FREE BONUSES BELOW!

Free Bonus Offer: Get Free Access To The PotentialRise.com VIP Newsletter!

Once you enter your email address you will immediately get free access to this awesome newsletter!

But wait, right now if you join now for free you will also get free access to the "LIMITLESS ENERGY" free EBook!

To claim both your FREE VIP NEWSLETTER MEMBERSHIP and your FREE BONUS Ebook on LIMITLESS ENERGY!

Just Go To:

www.PotentialRise.com

Made in the USA
Middletown, DE
05 March 2018